About Rodents

For the One who created rodents.

—*Genesis* 1:25

Ω

Published by
PEACHTREE PUBLISHERS
1700 Chattahoochee Avenue
Atlanta, Georgia 30318-2112
www.peachtree-online.com

Text © 2008 by Cathryn P. Sill
Illustrations © 2008 by John C. Sill

Illustrations created in watercolor on archival quality 100% rag watercolor paper
Text and titles set in Novarese from Adobe Systems

Printed in China
10 9 8 7 6 5 4 3 2

Library of Congress Cataloging-in-Publication Data

Sill, Cathryn P., 1953-
  About rodents : a guide for children / written by Cathryn Sill ; illustrated by John Sill.
-- 1st ed.
      p. cm.
  ISBN-13: 978-1-56145-454-9 / ISBN-10: 1-56145-454-0
  1. Rodents--Juvenile literature. I. Sill, John, ill. II. Title.
  QL737.R6S587 2008
  599.35--dc22   2-4-09
                            2008004558

About Rodents

A Guide for Children

Cathryn Sill

Illustrated by John Sill

PEACHTREE
ATLANTA

Rodents are mammals with special front
teeth that never stop growing.

PLATE 1
North American Porcupine

Rodents keep their front teeth short and sharp by gnawing on hard things.

Rodents live almost everywhere.

Their homes may be under the ground…

PLATE 4
Black-tailed Prairie Dog

on the ground…

PLATE 5
White-throated Woodrat

in trees...

PLATE 6
Eurasian Red Squirrel

in water...

or sometimes in the places where we live.

PLATE 8
House Mouse

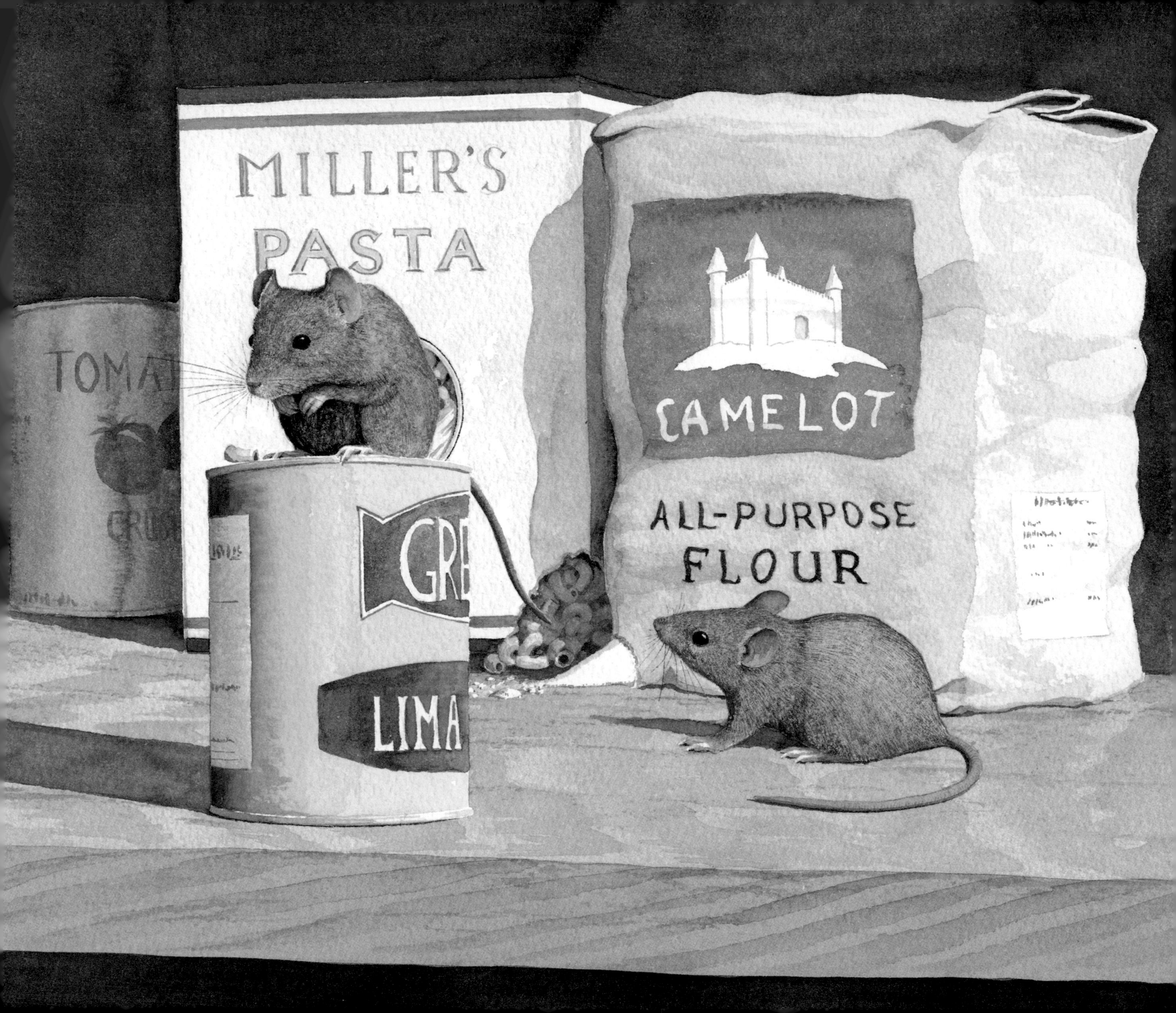
MILLER'S
PASTA
CAMELOT
ALL-PURPOSE
FLOUR
LIMA

Most rodents eat plants.

PLATE 9
Woodchuck

Some eat plants, insects, and other small animals.

Some rodents have stretchy cheek pouches, which they use to carry food to their dens.

Others hide food in different places, then come back for it later.

Some rodents that live in cold areas eat a lot in summer and fall. They get fat so they can hibernate in winter.

Most rodents are small.

PLATE 14
Eurasian Harvest Mouse

A few are big.

PLATE 15
Capybara

Many rodents have short lives. They have large families that grow up quickly to take their places.

PLATE 16
Golden Hamster

Rodents provide food for many predators.

PLATE 17
Barn Owl with Brown Rat

Rodents and the places where they live are important and should be protected.

Afterword

PLATE 1
There are around 2,000 species of rodents in the world. They make up more than 40 percent of the world's mammals. Rodents use their large incisors to chew tough foods, dig burrows, and gnaw through objects such as roots that get in their way. In winter North American Porcupines chew through the rough outer bark of trees so they can eat the inner bark. The North American Porcupine is North America's second largest rodent.

PLATE 2
The front surfaces of a rodent's incisors are covered with hard enamel. The backs of the incisors are soft and wear down faster. This keeps the teeth sharp. Many rodents gnaw on antlers shed by deer. The gnawing sharpens their incisors, and at the same time the discarded antlers provide them with calcium and other minerals. White-footed Deermice are common in forests and brushy areas in the eastern United States.

PLATE 3
Rodents are found in almost every habitat on Earth. Harris's Antelope Squirrels are common in the Sonoran desert of North America. Northern Collared Lemmings live in the Arctic tundra, farther north than any other North American rodent. Black Agoutis live in tropical forests in South America. Common Muskrats are found in marshes over most of the United States and Canada. Hispid Cotton Rats live in grassy fields and overgrown pastures in southeastern North America and Central America.

PLATE 4

Rodents need shelter where they can sleep, store food, raise babies, and hide from predators. Black-tailed Prairie Dogs dig burrows with rooms linked together by tunnels. Some of the rooms are "living rooms" and others are for storage or for toilets. The dirt removed from the burrows is piled around the entrances to keep the tunnels from flooding during heavy rains. Prairie dogs also use the mounds as lookouts where they can watch for predators. Black-tailed Prairie Dogs live in the great plains of North America.

PLATE 5

Rodents need ways to keep their nests on the ground safe. White-throated Woodrats build nests of sticks and cactus pieces under cholla and prickly pear cactuses. The cactus spines protect them from predators. Woodrats are also called packrats or trade rats. They collect a variety of small objects to put in their nests. They will often drop what they are carrying and trade it for something else. White-throated Woodrats live in brushlands and deserts in the southwestern United States.

PLATE 6

Holes in tree trunks and high branches provide safe places for some rodents to build nests. Tree squirrels are able to move quickly along the branches and trunks of trees. Good eyesight helps them judge distances as they leap from branch to branch. Eurasian Red Squirrels find shelter in holes in tree trunks or in round nests they build from twigs. They line the nests with soft material such as moss, dried grass, or thistledown. Eurasian Red Squirrels live in forests in Europe and Asia.

PLATE 7

Beavers are able to change their environment to make safe places for their homes. North American Beavers use their sharp teeth to cut trees and branches for building dams across streams. The dams cause deep ponds to form, where the beavers can build stick and mud nests called lodges. The entrances to the lodges are underwater, which helps keep predators out. In some areas where the water is deep enough, beavers dig burrows in the banks of rivers and lakes. Beavers are North America's largest rodent.

PLATE 8

House Mice have lived close to people for thousands of years. They can live almost anywhere because they eat almost anything. House Mice can be pests when they live in buildings because they get into food, gnaw on furnishings, and carry disease. Outdoors, though, they can be helpful because they eat weed seeds and insects that destroy crops. House Mice spread all over the world when they were accidentally carried on the ships or wagons used by explorers and settlers. They are found in all but the very coldest parts of the world.

PLATE 9

Different kinds of rodents eat different parts of plants. Woodchucks—or groundhogs—eat grasses, green leaves, buds, and twigs. When woodchucks are frightened, they make a shrill squeal that sounds like a whistle. Because of this, some people call them "whistle pigs." Woodchucks live in the eastern United States and throughout most of Canada.

PLATE 10

Southern Flying Squirrels hunt for food at night. They eat many things, including nuts, seeds, berries, tree sap, fungi, insects, smaller animals, bird eggs, and carrion. Flying Squirrels have special folds of skin on their sides that help them glide from tree to tree. Southern Flying Squirrels live in the eastern United States and in parts of Mexico and Central America.

PLATE 11

Rodents have ways to survive times when food is scarce. In late summer and fall Eastern Chipmunks gather and store enough food to last them through the winter. They carry large amounts of seeds and nuts to their burrows in cheek pouches. When full, the cheek pouches are nearly as big as their skulls. Eastern Chipmunks live in eastern United States and southeastern Canada.

PLATE 12

Eastern Gray Squirrels prepare for winter by burying extra nuts in many places. Their good sense of smell helps the squirrels find the nuts when they return to dig them up. Some of the hidden nuts are never found and grow into trees. Eastern Gray Squirrels are native to eastern North America but have been introduced to parts of Europe and South Africa.

PLATE 13

Some rodents, like many other animals, hibernate in winter when food is hard to find. A hibernating animal eats a lot in the late summer and early fall, then goes into a deep sleep and lives off the fat stored in its body. Hazel Dormice may hibernate from October to April. They build nests in shrubby areas in woods throughout most of Europe.

PLATE 14

Eurasian Harvest Mice are one of the smallest rodents. They can easily climb thin stems of wheat, reeds, or grass. They use their prehensile tails as well as their feet to help them climb. Eurasian Harvest Mice weave blades of grass together to make a nest about the size of a tennis ball. They live in Europe and Asia.

PLATE 15

Capybaras are the largest rodents in the world. They can weigh up to 145 pounds. Capybaras have partly webbed feet that help them swim well. They can swim under water and stay submerged up to five minutes. Capybaras eat grasses and other plants that grow in and around water. These large rodents live near rivers and lakes in South America.

PLATE 16

Small mouselike rodents have shorter life spans than larger rodents such as beavers that can live up to 20 years. Golden Hamsters live for 2 to 2 1/2 years. They usually have 5 to 10 babies in a litter but have been known to have up to 20. The babies are weaned from their mother's milk by the time they are 3 weeks old. Golden Hamsters are also called Syrian Hamsters. Even though they are common pets, Golden Hamsters are endangered in the wild. They live in a very small area of Syria in southwest Asia.

PLATE 17

Rodents are the most numerous mammals in the world partly because of their high birth rate. Each day millions of rodents become prey for other animals. Many mammals, birds, and reptiles depend on rodents for food. Some farmers provide nest sites for Barn Owls, which help control rodent pests that destroy crops. Barn Owls and Brown Rats are widespread throughout most of the world.

PLATE 18

Rodents are an important part of the animal world and are beneficial in many ways. Some types of rodents are used for medical research. Some eat harmful insects and weed seeds. Rodents provide food for people in some places. They make popular pets. Long-tailed Chinchillas do well in captivity and are often kept as pets. They are very rare in the wild because they were trapped for their soft warm fur. Wild chinchillas are now protected by law, but their numbers continue to decline because of illegal hunting and habitat destruction. Long-tailed Chinchillas live on cold rocky slopes of the Andes Mountains in South America.

GLOSSARY

Carrion—dead and decaying flesh
Environment—the surroundings of an animal or plant
Habitat—the place where an animal or plant lives and grows
Hibernate—to go into a deep sleep during cold weather
Incisors—teeth in the front of the mouth used for cutting
Mammal—an animal that feeds its babies milk
Predator—an animal that lives by hunting and eating other animals
Prey—an animal that is hunted and eaten by a predator
Prehensile—adapted for grasping and holding
Species—a group of closely related animals or plants

BIBLIOGRAPHY

BOOKS

Rodents from Rats to Muskrats by Sara Swan Miller (Franklin Watts)
Looking at Small Mammals: Rodents by Sally Morgan (Chrysalis Education)
Guinea Pigs and Other Rodents by Bobbie Kalman and Reagan Miller (Crabtree Publishing Company)
World of Animals Vol. 7 *Mammals: Rodents 1* by Pat Morris and Amy-Jane Beer (Grolier)
World of Animals Vol. 8 *Mammals: Rodents 2 and Lagomorphs* by Pat Morris and Amy-Jane Beer (Grolier)

WEBSITES

http://www.americazoo.com/goto/index/mammals/rodentia.htm
http://kids.nationalgeographic.com/Stories/WackyStories/Ratatouille
http://www.the-piedpiper.co.uk/th1.htm

Also in the About… series

ABOUT THE SILLS

Cathryn Sill, a former elementary school teacher, is the author of the acclaimed ABOUT… series. With her husband John and her brother-in-law Ben Sill, she coauthored the popular bird-guide parodies, A FIELD GUIDE TO LITTLE-KNOWN AND SELDOM-SEEN BIRDS OF NORTH AMERICA, ANOTHER FIELD GUIDE TO LITTLE-KNOWN AND SELDOM-SEEN BIRDS OF NORTH AMERICA, and BEYOND BIRDWATCHING, all from Peachtree Publishers.

John Sill is a prize-winning and widely published wildlife artist. He illustrated the ABOUT… series and coauthored and illustrated the FIELD GUIDES and BEYOND BIRDWATCHING. A native of North Carolina, he holds a B.S. in Wildlife Biology from North Carolina State University.

The Sills live and work in Franklin, North Carolina.

Fred Eldredge, Creative Image Photography

Books in the ABOUT… series

ISBN 978-1-56145-028-2 HC
ISBN 978-1-56145-147-0 PB

ISBN 978-1-56145-141-8 HC
ISBN 978-1-56145-174-6 PB

ISBN 978-1-56145-183-8 HC
ISBN 978-1-56145-233-0 PB

ISBN 978-1-56145-207-1 HC
ISBN 978-1-56145-232-3 PB

ISBN 978-1-56145-234-7 HC
ISBN 978-1-56145-312-2 PB

ISBN 978-1-56145-256-9 HC
ISBN 978-1-56145-335-1 PB

ISBN 978-1-56145-038-1 HC
ISBN 978-1-56145-364-1 PB

ISBN 978-1-56145-301-6 HC
ISBN 978-1-56145-405-1 PB

ISBN 978-1-56145-331-3 HC
ISBN 978-1-56145-406-8 PB

ISBN 978-1-56145-358-0 HC